This is how we **do it!**

Characteristics of Effective Learning in Early Years

by Kirstine Beeley

Cover design by Stephanie Breen
Book design by Design Dejour –www.design-dejour.co.uk

Published by Playing to Learn, Kirstine Beeley – www.playingtolearnuk.com

ISBN 978-0-9955315-0-5

Photography courtesy of Treehouse Pre-School, Winslow, Buckingham Park C of E Primary School, Aylesbury and Prestwood Primary School, Buckinghamshire

Printed by Diverze Print Limited www.diverze.com
11 Ropa Court, Leighton Buzzard, Bedfordshire LU7 1DU

Printed in Great Britain

Contents

Introduction

In 2008 the then UK government introduced the EYFS (Early Years Foundation Stage) to England with the subsequent introduction of early years frameworks in Wales, Scotland and Northern Ireland. Within the pages of the statutory guidance on Early Years provision for children aged 0-5 years was mention of not only what children were expected to learn but how they could learn best. The update of the EYFS in 2014 and its sister support document Development Matters (2014) coined the phrase "Characteristics of Effective Learning" to incorporate best practice in early years provision.

Covering three main areas – Playing and Exploring, Active Learning and Creativity and Critical Thinking, the Characteristics of Effective Learning (CoEL) place emphasis on the process of learning rather than a product or outcome. Their focus being on helping children to develop both the skills and attitudes needed to become confident individuals with a lifelong love of learning. Yet over the last few years many practitioners have taken the headings and subheadings encompassed by the CoEL and used them almost as a "tick list" approach to checking what children are doing. They should however, in my opinion, be used as a guide to how, rather than what, we get children to learn and as a direct result of that they should be viewed as being more about the many influencing factors in developing effective, confident learners than a can or cannot do assessment. In summary, within the EYFS, Characteristics of Effective Learning are the HOW and the Learning and Development headings are the WHAT.

For the purposes of this book I aim to break down the CoEL within the EYFS for practitioners and look at each heading and subheading in more depth. Looking at how they influence what we provide in good early years settings, covering everything from the physical environments to adult-child interactions, partnerships with parents and more. For those of you reading from outside of England, I strongly believe that these headings and the subsequent discussion and ideas can be transposed into any good, child led, inquiry based early learning environment and are hence interchangeable with other frameworks. Focusing on lifelong learning skills there is no reason why many of the principles and ideas cannot be used with other older age groups.

I hope in writing this book, to draw upon 10 years of experience as an Early Years training provider combined with 24 years of teaching experience to offer ideas and suggestions to help you in your own journey towards providing engaging, enabling early years learning environments. As an active teacher-practitioner I will aim to offer examples gleaned from different settings in both state school and private sectors, but predominantly from Treehouse Pre-School where I

have for the past eight years been parent, chairperson, key person and teacher and where I am happy to say Ofsted have awarded us Outstanding in all areas in 2015. I would like to thank the staff, parents, children and mostly Sarah the manager for their time and patience as I continually provide them with new ideas for their reflective practice. Without them this book would not exist.

Please take from this book what works best for you. My belief that all children are unique individuals and hence all settings are uniquely different means that what works for one setting may not work for your own. However, my passion for what good early years practice looks like remains unchanged and for that I make no apologies. I hope you find something useful within these pages and enjoy it as much as I have enjoyed writing it.

Playing & Exploring

Finding out and exploring

Enabling environments

For children to learn effectively they need to really want to learn. We as practitioners need to tap into children's natural curiosity and look to find ways of exciting their imaginations. Before any learning can take place our emphasis has to be on how to develop supportive environments that actively encourage inquiry and exploration. In Reggio styled settings the environment is viewed as the "third teacher", an active participant in the learning process and there is much that we can do to make sure our own settings become "can't keep my hands off" learning environments.

Space

Young children need space to explore, to work through ideas and to really engage with their environment. A room full of tables and chairs offers little opportunity to move, to extend or to be creative. Young children tend to prefer to work at low level naturally and hence removing table height furniture and opting for a less cluttered feel where children are able to access comfortable floor space can lead to them feeling more relaxed, more comfortable and more able to follow their own ideas. Try to keep what furniture you do have to low level play surfaces where children can gain easy access and essentials such as snack table and creative surfaces. There is no requirement in EYFS to have one chair for every child and adding chairs to some areas can even be counterproductive. Chairs at a playdough bar stop children from pushing down from shoulders and using back muscles essential in pre-writing physical development.

If in doubt take a few minutes to sit back and watch your children and see where they naturally play. We have found that low level tables are great and cheap – painting one of ours with blackboard paint has given old furniture a new lease of play life. When creating learning spaces, less is definitely more in early years!

That said, young children also need small, cosy spaces where they can feel secure, creating these within your setting is also essential. Young children are more likely to want to build good communication skills when they have tailored environments, where they feel secure and relaxed. There are many ways to create cosy talk spaces such as rose arches with drapes, play tents and even under the tables you will no longer be using as working surfaces! Remember to add lots of cushions and material to make them extra magical and enticing from a child perspective.

Home from home

Tastes and trends vary when it comes to how to present your setting with some opting for bright and colourful while others go for a paired-down version. I am an advocate of the latter as I have found over the years that neutral tones and earthy colours make settings look and feel calmer and more relaxing and do not detract from the learning resources and experiences on offer. Too many bright colours and displays and children can sometimes become over stimulated and less able to filter the background from the important learning they are trying to access. With often clinical institutionalised buildings

at our disposal there is much that can be done cheaply to soften environments to make them more relaxing and appealing and less of an assault on the senses. Try using fabric to soften walls or dim harsh lighting (fire proof materials of course), or adding cushions, blankets, bean bags and soft furnishing to make areas cosy and appealing. Try and steer away from stringing loads of laminated bits and pieces across from one side of the room to the other. It just adds to the cluttered, confusing busy-ness of the room. No child ever stopped their play, when fully engaged and excited, and commented on the number line or birthday months hanging way above their heads (even if they are double laminated!).

The EYFS accepts parents as children's primary educators (EYFS 2014) and as such we as practitioners must acknowledge that much of the children's learning happens in a home

Before

environment. If we can recreate a more relaxed, home-like environment then transition into our settings becomes smoother for children and they are able to continue accessing learning in a more familiar environment. I always advocate the addition of a sofa where possible to encourage children to sit and talk, or read with peers and adults in a home from home relaxed way. Soft rugs encourage children to work on open floor spaces and invite them to engage with resources nearby.

Independence and access

For young children to truly feel they have ownership of their own learning and ideas, they have to have ownership of their choices. There is much that we can do to our environments to support and encourage independent choices and build confidence in children's own ability to lead their learning. Children need to feel confident and able to choose resources and activities, knowing that adults will support those choices and allow them to pan out in the child's own time. Having smaller amounts of key resources, stored in open top baskets or clear trays, allows children to know instantly where things are. With a little support they themselves are able to take them out when they want to explore them. This means a move away from "displays" of resources (usually adult created), where children are discouraged from interacting with its components let alone encouraged to move them elsewhere.

We need to provide access to resources that are flexible in their use and can be taken to the children's learning rather than the children having to come to the resources. Magnifying glasses need to be taken to where the minibeast has been found instead of being on a table with the sole purpose of looking at the object the teacher has chosen today. In good child led early learning environments it is alright for the babies in the role play area to end up in the water tray having a bath or for the dinosaurs to be exploring the sand tray. Controversially I am an advocate of not labelling draws and baskets. I believe

excite...engage...explore...enhance...extend

that there are many more opportunities for children to access text that are more relevant and engaging (see 'What they know' section). I have found over the years that using more open-ended resources, getting less hung up on whether things are back in exactly the right box, has led to practitioners relaxing more about the environment and engaging more in the children's play. Of course using the "Choose, Use it, Put it away" mantra to encourage a sense of shared ownership with even very young children helps to minimise damage and mis-use of resources, but

there will always be an element of resetting your environment – but that's just early years!

Having said that, for children to build independence in their use of resources they do often find it useful to have centralised areas where they know they can find things. I believe it is fine to have an area where children know they can find maths-based measuring equipment or science enquiry resources as long as provision is not limited to use in these areas. Maths does after all happen in all areas and not just in a "maths area". Make sure you have access to writing and reading materials in all areas too.

Engage and excite

Once you have the basic structure of your environment sorted with space to explore, you will need to be looking at how exciting your offering is from a child's perspective. Does an activity or area scream "come and play with me" or is it bland, uninviting and uninspiring? How often have you just taken the lid off your sand tray with little thought for what might be available to use in it? Or filled your water tray with water and wondered why no one came to play with it? Thought has to go into what is available and how interesting and exciting it looks to the children. So, as well as your everyday (or continuous) provision, we have to make sure there are lots of open ended and engaging additions to the setting. We need to be developing "invitations to play" that draw the children in and invite them to explore and tap into their natural curiosity.

Sensory stimulation

In early childhood children explore the world around them with all of their senses. Every time they experience something new they develop new brain connections, which will become the building blocks for their lifelong learning. The more we excite and stimulate the senses, the more the children's brains will be "firing and rewiring". With this in mind we need to develop our settings so that children are actively encouraged to explore with all of their senses. From using light panels to interact with fruit and veg to including scented playdough or rainbow coloured rice the need to stimulate sensory exploration is vital in early learning.

Treasure to measure.

Take sand play as a great example. Many of the resources freely available for purchase to use in sand are plastic and as such offer only one sensory experience. That of sight – as one plastic object held in a hand feels the same in texture and temperature as the next plastic object. Developing a collection of vessels and objects made from a variety of metals (treasure to measure – see picture) gives loads of open ended access to maths talk and problem-solving whilst offering a huge array of textures, temperature and sensory experiences. The same can be said for loads of natural materials and objects and hence filling your setting with as many natural elements as you can also increases the amount of sensory explorations available to children.

Sensory herbs.

o make things really exciting you can then
tart to look at what the children's interests are
nd use these as a starting point to think about
nhancing your environment to produce maximum
ngagement for the children. Work on the basis that
any area or activity makes you say "wow", it may
vell interest the children.

Don't forget to
offer sensory stimulation
indoors and outdoors
– cinnamon in sand or
mint and basil in the mud
kitchen are great ways of
increasing the children's
access to smell.

excite...engage...explore...enhance...extend

Playing with what they know

Children use what they see at home as their starting point for play, and hence for learning. A child will happily replicate their parent talking on a phone or baking a cake as they play in a home corner, this type of play is really important to learning development. It acts as a pre-cursor to imaginative story play. Children naturally move from playing with a real phone to talk to Dad, to using a building block or a banana as a phone to pretend play; all the time building their imaginative play and story telling abilities. What we sometimes need to remember, when we are on our quest for the holy grail of early writing, is that

being an author is not just about the physical act of putting pencil to paper – it has its roots in storytelling. Children need opportunities to explore and build storylines, develop characters, act out speeches and all of this comes from imaginative play. Children make sense of their own world by revisiting it in their play and are able to explore feelings and emotions within a safe framework. So exploring with "real" things is an essential part of the early learning process and builds children's confidence to extend and explore using what they already know as a base.

et if playing with what they know is so key to their early learning then we **must** reflect what they know in our settings. As practitioners we need to know what, and with who the children play and interact with at home. We need to know their likes and dislikes, their natural preferences and their interests. We need to know what they know so we can help them revisit it!

Children's interests as a tool for invitations to play.

What interests and excites the children!

Children's interests displays

One of the first steps to child interest-led inquiry is to assess what the children's interests and preferences are. My advice is to display this somewhere prominent for all practitioner to see. Knowing what interests children have and being able to see if you have a cohort with similar interests, will help to guide what enhancements you add to your setting to develop even more engagement and exploration. If you find you have half a dozen children who really like dinosaurs, then you know you need make sure your dinosaurs are topped up and easily accessible. If your children seem to be developing an innate knowledge of a particular TV or film character you will find that reflecting these interests in your setting can stimulate added enthusiasm and excitement.

That's not to say that you just need loads of TV character play figures (although these are amazing at helping children to develop small word imaginative play scenarios). Interests and popular culture can be reflected in many other ways around your setting. Jigsaws and games can often be found with Disney or TV characters on. Books and comics offer a great introduction to reading for a reason and can provide ample opportunity to explore page turning, picture discussions and more early-reading skills. Superheroes in the spaghetti with scissors is a great way of getting little hands cutting, and freezing characters from Disney or Marvel in ice can act as an amazing starting point for early-talking and problem solving. Note, these are **enhancements** to provision you already have in place, to help build on excitement, curiosity and the children's likelihood of engaging with the environment. They are NOT tasks for children to be pulled away from their play to visit with an adult.

Enhancing your environment with what children know does not stop at fictional characters or an obsession with trains or planes. We can reflect children's own lives and experiences across the setting to give them even more opportunities to reflect and revisit their first hand experiences.

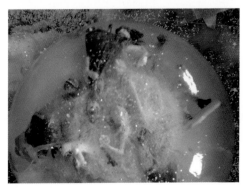

Environmental print alphabet.

Making reading real

For young children to be able to read they first need to understand that text carries meaning. In a world where they are surrounded by logos and printed text this has to be our first port of call when enhancing our environments. We need to look at what the children see on a daily or weekly basis and reflect that in our settings. So in the home corner we need lots of examples of real text. Add cereal packets and real tins, washing up bottles, baby milk tins and empty furniture spray cans. All have huge potential for children to copy what they see at home in their play at the same time as recognising familiar logos (reading in its earliest and easiest form!).

As well as the packets and tins, try adding magazines and comics in places such as reading nooks and snack tables. Try creating a logo wall of familiar packets and boxes or even an environmental print alphabet with loads of familiar logos for children to read. The more confident children get at recognising familiar text, the more confident they will become at having a go at reading unfamiliar text as they build their knowledge of letters and sounds.

Maths all around

The same approach of taking the child's real world and replicating in your own environment, helps when it comes to making maths understandable and real. Take time to reflect on all of the ways that maths impacts on children at home and make provision for these in their play. Add calculators, remote controls, mobile phones, rulers, clocks (digital and analogue), watches, baking scales, measuring jugs and spoons, dice, dominoe and playing cards to your continuous provision. Even when considering number lines try to make it "real" for the children. A number line made from birthday cards makes it much more exciting and relatable.

And then remember to look for the maths potential within children's play choices NOT bringing children out of their play to "do" maths. Loads of maths can come from making cakes in the mud kitchen, from pouring potions and from playing in the sand – but that's a whole other book!

Mini me's.

Local landmarks on building blocks.

excite...engage...explore...enhance...extend

"Real" small world

Try adding elements of the children's own lives into your small world imaginative play provision too. Adding pictures of familiar shops and places of interest to wooden building blocks adds local interest to your block play and gives children a chance to revisit events in their own lives as they play. Other similar additions include "mini me's" – cut outs of the children laminated for use in small world play and "staff lids" allowing children to add staff members into their play as well as talking about and revisiting significant events.

Staff lids.

Willing to have a go

This part of CoEL stems from children's own confidence. Their ability to try new things and overcome reservations. Exploring new and exciting experiences is rooted in how we, as adults, interact with the children. Do we let the children truly and freely explore or do we try to get them to do as we want them to do? Do we really listen to the children's ideas and respond at the time or do we stick to what we planned in tablets of stone? Are we fearful of the consequences should we veer from that planned path? Here the true nature of child led learning starts to impact not only on how you set up your environment but also on the way in which the adults concerned interact with the children to ensure learning occurs. This section challenges some of the traditional approaches to working with young children and hopefully offers an alternative to top down teaching methods.

Free choice and access

Having enabled our environment as discussed in the previous section of this book, with excitement and child interest in mind; it is now time to look at how we allow children access to these resources. Setting up so that children make their own choices at the beginning of a session leads not only to child initiated play from the off, but less effort in setting up for the adults. It leaves staff free to enhance with one off exciting invitations to play or to reset and restock free access areas. The focus shifts from setting up an array of activities to draw children towards, to enabling the environment to engage, excite and stimulate learning. Remember what we, as adults, see as a "good idea" or exciting is not necessarily what children see as engaging and appealing. Letting them decide what they play with and how they use it lets us as practitioners move away from the disappointment of preparing an activity for hours only to find no one was interested in it. It lets us embrace an exciting way of working where we know very little of what is about to unfold in front of us on any one chosen day but does not mean that learning does not occur. The difference is, we reflect on what has happened after the event and use these observations to lead any changes to our provision.

Furniture for free play

For children to be able to access resources and make independent choices we need to carefully consider our furniture and how we lay out our offering. Are our units open enough to offer ease of access, can children see what's in containers? Are trays/baskets too heavy for children to be able to move them to where they choose to play? In this instance less is definitely more. A few carefully chosen resources offered in an exciting accessible way is much more appealing, and hence more likely to be played with, than a tonne of resources all in heavy drawers that children cannot get out. Or so much stuff that they just don't know where to begin. Using baskets displayed on shelves rather than plastic trays, offer another sensory addition to your setting and gives a light, easily movable option for children. Try using baskets on the floor for low level access to books and other resources.

There is lots to consider when looking at cupboards and surfaces too. Are they too high for children to reach? Are shelves too deep for children to see what is in them? Do they offer the opportunity to create inviting spaces where children are able to develop their own ideas unhindered by others? Or conversely is there space between pieces to let ideas grow and expand? My advice would be to try things, watch how children use the area and then tweak it if needs be. No setting, even the outstanding ones, is ever perfect! Good, reflective practitioners are always looking for ways to enhance and extend their setting based on ever changing children's interests and ever growing children.

Adult as facilitator

When children know that it is alright for them to choose their own play resources they often look to the adults around them for help in enhancing their play. The adults' role becomes less of a teacher and more of a facilitator. Adults need to observe children in their choices and know when to sensitively intervene in order to take the play forward to offer options for enhancing learning. Sensitivity being the key here, as any child, when playing with a favourite toy or engrossed in their imaginative world, will not take lightly to you crashing in asking "how many dinosaurs have you got there then?". Adults become the means by which children find the resources – they need to build a bridge across their railway, or to add more exciting ingredients to their potion to turn everyone green! Our role is to listen really carefully and to offer assistance when needed. Adults become the means by which children explore and access their own ideas and extend their own thinking. The more a child knows you will support them in their choices, the more confident they become in making more exciting choices; and the more likely they are to explore new situations.

Open ended resources

What you actually give children to play with can have a huge impact on their confidence to make choices and explore their own ideas. Offering open-ended resources, where there is no right or wrong way of using them, frees children up to be creative in their thinking and more adventurous in their choices. Stock your setting with an array of materials so that children are always free to explore and use them in their own way. Examples of open ended resources are:

Indoors...

Pine cones, glass gems, sticks, pots, fabric samples, artificial grass squares, wooden curtain rings and stands, nuts and bolts, pebbles, shells, cardboard tubes and wooden blocks.

Outdoors...

Pine cones, shells, log slices, guttering, drain pipes, milk/bread crates, tubing and hose pieces, bricks, blocks, tyres, logs and bottle babies (large plastic bottles filled with coloured water and sealed – children carry them like babies!).

Open ended resources not only encourage children to build and explore what their heart desires but also lessen the need for time consuming set up. Freely accessible resources can be left out or easily stored as they often cost no money at all.

Remember to keep topping up your stock of loose parts to maintain interest and maximise creativity.

excite...engage...explore...enhance...exten

excite...engage...explore...enhance...exten

Risk/benefit assessment

Encouraging children to "have a go" means we do have to sometimes let go of our traditional approach to health and safety and assess whether the benefits of a choice to lift something heavy or to climb a tree or a piece of equipment will outweigh any risk. In a world where legislation attempts to wrap children in cotton wool and protect them from any risk, we need to ask ourselves how we are preparing our children to make safe choices and to take risks with their thinking. So I would urge you next time a child decides to try and walk along a metal rail to consider "are they really going to hurt themselves if I watch carefully?", i.e. will me letting them work out how to move in and out of the rails give them key physical development skills, as well as building on problem-solving and their all-important confidence?. It is a decision that needs to be made "in the moment" and with safety obviously at the forefront, but may free you from all the "no you can't do that" and take you to a place where "let's have a go and see" becomes more the norm.

Importance of revisiting

For children to build confidence in their own abilities and the courage they need to try new things, we also need to provide them with the opportunity to revisit activities. To re-try things they were once not confident enough to have a go at and also to re-do things they succeeded at previously. Revisiting is an important theme which runs throughout this book and is key to accessing Characteristics of Effective Learning in so many ways. In this instance the ability to revisit when they may not have been so confident the first time allows children to grow in an environment where they know their choices are supported. The idea of revisiting is at the heart of continuous provision and means children become increasingly more familiar and confident to use the resources provided, rather than a succession of pre-planned activities available only for one day. The more children are able to revisit their choices, the more confident they will become in making new choices and having a go at new ways of thinking.

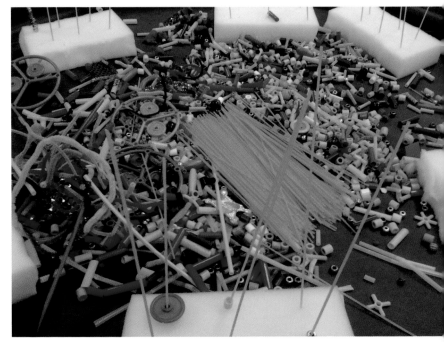

excite...engage...explore...enhance...exten

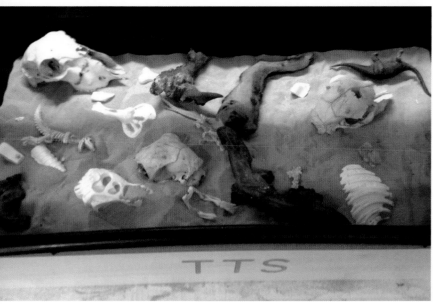

Active Learning

Being involved and concentrating

Once children are engaged with an activity we really want them to, sustain their interest, getting really involved in what they are doing. It is when they are in this heightened state of interaction and thinking, that brain connections really begin to fire and learning truly develops. Hence, the importance of developing an environment which really hooks their interest and reels them in to develop their own ideas. From a practitioner point of view we need to be watching the children and looking for those moments when they are concentrating on something to the exclusion of the outside world. I find photographs are a great way of capturing this moment and when displayed show others what to look for (see opposite). If however, our children lower level interest in activities and are approaching with a "pick up, look, drop" approach then we will need to reassess and re-adjust what we are providing. Rethinking whether it is of interest to the children and whether it offers them enough scope to explore and develop their own ideas.

Time and space to explore and revisit

Being deeply engaged with an activity is not the be all and end all of this aspect of CoEL. Children also need the time to stay focused on an activity of choice. To really get into what they are doing and see their ideas through to a natural conclusion. This need for time to explore comes in contrast to traditional school timetabling and best practice requires a rethink of breaks for P.E. or playtime. Would our children be better served if, instead of leaving what they are engrossed in, to join in with play on a big playground (often with much bigger children where the noise levels can be overwhelming). Or would we rather they stay focused on their play and carry on with their sustained thinking? Just because we have done things a certain way for 30 years does not necessarily make it the best way to still do things!

As well as time to explore and to get really involved in what they are doing children also need the space to think things through themselves. Adults need to be mindful of interrupting children when they are in this fully focused state. Only interrupt if absolutely necessary or if you think your input will help the child to take their thinking forward. Sometimes children are best left alone to explore the world with a watchful adult on hand if needed.

Child led versus adult imposed

One common misconception about EYFS is that the balance required of child initiated and adult led learning requires practitioners to plan specific activities to draw children away in small groups to complete a task. THIS IS NOT THE CASE. Adult input is much better placed if it is in reaction to a child's own initiated interest. The adult then takes up the mantle to enhance and extend the learning. In this way the children are involved and engaged at every stage, rather than removing them from something they have chosen to be fully involved in. It is, for example, the difference between a group of children being asked to sit and classify a group of minibeasts according to legs etc. and an adult working with children who have found a bug to see if they can work out what it is using reference books, internet etc. to reach a classification. In child led settings the adult still has input into learning but lets the child guide them as to where that input is needed to extend their thinking. In other words the adults look for the learning and goes to where the children are rather and trying to drag the children to the learning. Taking away the need for adult planned activities leaves practitioners free to plan how to enhance their environments with exciting invitations to play.

Sometimes a child is best left alone to explore.

Look for the learning

For adult interventions and assessments to be of value, practitioners need to know what to look for. We need to be confident in what learning is expected of children and look for opportunities to involve the language needed within the children's play. I would suggest revisiting the Early Learning Goals for EYFS and using the Development Matters documentation as a team to unpick the language you really want the children to be using, in all areas of learning and development. Agree what you should be looking out for and the language you want to be using. This way everyone knows what is expected and can support each other in looking for the learning in all children. Then you can go out and try to look for instances when the language can be used and extended within the children's play. It is important to remember that with a child led, inquiry based setting lots of learning will come from one child initiated activity. Rather than only one learning objective from an adult planned-adult led activity. A great example of this is when children play within a mud kitchen environment.

Mud kitchen play

A well-resourced mud kitchen with lots of different sized and shaped containers, pots and pans with access to a variety of smelly herbs, a water source and of course lots of mud, can offer huge learning potential.

Playing imaginatively in the first place as they pretend to bake cakes, make tea etc. develops language and communication skills between children and confidence to explore imaginative story telling skills. When mixing and making with mud children naturally explore capacity and weight as they measure and scoop, and number makes

more sense when you are deciding if you need one more or one less piece of mud pizza. Addin extra ingredients such as herbs encourages children to explore the language of smell and to talk about likes and dislikes freely in their play. A few real vegetables such as carrots and potatoes offer a great first hand opportunity to explore size and shape at the same time as developing fine motor skills. All this learning car be observed and supported by an adult if they know what they are looking for!

Keeping on trying

This part of CoEL is what some practitioners refer to as resilience. A child's ability to bounce back from something not going to plan and to try again until they succeed. And like other areas of CoEL its success depends on sensitive adult interactions. To develop confident, independent and resilient children we need to sometimes rethink how we interact with the children as they try to work things out for themselves. Does your setting actively promote independence? Are choices made by children rather than adults? Are children given the time and space to try things for themselves? How well do we make provision for developing independence?

Doing it for myself

A long time ago I was introduced to this saying which has stayed with me as an important reminder of why we, as practitioners, need to let children try themselves. Even if we desperately want to help them or we are in a hurry to get something done.

If you;
Cut it,
Stick it,
Write it,
Paint it,
For me...
All that I learn is that you can do it better than me.

Source unknown

It is really important that we, as adults, take time to stand back and let children work things out for themselves. There is a fine line between helping and interfering. Giving encouragement and support without actually taking over can be a difficult line to tread. But ultimately children will grow in confidence as they learn to stay determined and eventually succeed with their new found independence.

Planning for independence

That said, there is much that we can do to plan for independence within our early years settings. Looking at every aspect of our provision and asking ourselves "how can we get children to do this independently?" can lead to some minor, but significant, changes.

Children can, with encouragement, be helped to access many aspects of early years on their own. Even the very youngest of pre-school children can select their own drinks, wash their hands, put their coat on, get their own playdough and even mix their own paint colour

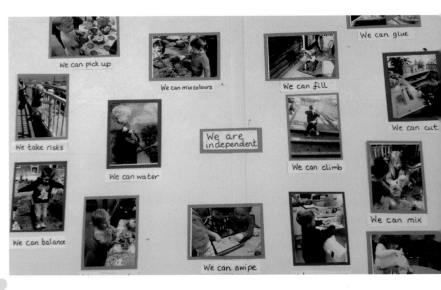

If you;   draw it for me,
         cut it for me,
         stick it for me,
all I learn is that YOU
can do it better than ME !!

Sophie   Jan 2016
"Mummy as a
ballerina."

Snails by Pippa

nack area

y providing easy to use tools
ongs build physical hand strength
nd co-ordination as well as giving
dependent access) children are able
 self select fruit and bread. Picture
ues can help and provide prompts for
aths talk as well. Using knives to butter
ur own toast and pouring our own
ater or milk all builds on children's
onfidence and independence. Adding
 washing up bowl gives them even
ore opportunity to do things for
emselves and builds a shared sense of
wnership in the setting.

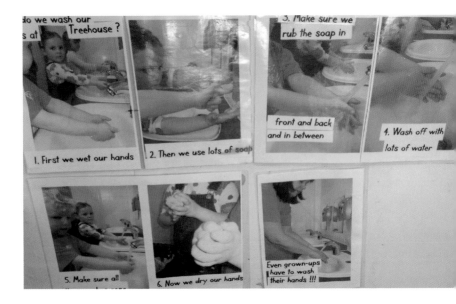

do we wash our ___
s at | Treehouse?

1. First we wet our hands

2. Then we use lots of soap

3. Make sure we rub the soap in

front and back and in between

4. Wash off with lots of water

5. Make sure all

6. Now we dry our hands

Even grown-ups have to wash their hands !!!

Routine prompts

Using picture prompts for key routines such as hand washing can encourage children to be independent. Use your own children in pictures to add to the shared sense of belonging and inclusion.

Why not rethink your playdough offering and see if you can make it suitable for independent access?

The right tools and the right attitude

Providing children with tools that let them follow their own ideas independently has a huge impact on how much they will try and do on their own. Even very young children can learn to easily use a tape dispenser, scissors, glue, self service paint bottles and even hammers and nails. The focus for the adult in these instances shifts from being the one to do the task, to being the one to share the skill with the child. You move from doing it for them to helping them to do it for themselves. All of this of course requires the adults concerned to have high expectations of the children and their abilities. Try not to avoid letting children do something because you think they will make a mess or use everything up. In my experience if you have high expectations children will not disappoint!

And of course make sure that you celebrate this independence and the subsequent resilience and not wanting to give up trying.

Enjoying achieving what they set out to do

Once children know that they can try out their own ideas, are supported in their choices and have the tools available to explore and experiment they then begin thoroughly enjoying the process of learning. The process becomes the important part of the journey and children begin to enjoy the process of mastering a skill rather than feeling they have to produce something praise worthy at the end. This again can only come from sensitive adult support and interaction whilst the process is in place. Sometimes is it worth sitting

excite...engage...explore...enhance...exten

ack and thinking how often do I praise what the child is doing rather than what they re producing? It is the difference between "Ooo what a lovely picture" and "Wow! I love he way you have mixed the colours to make the sky in your picture". Taking time to djust your interactions in this way to focus on the process, will in time show children hat they don't have to produce an end product to gain praise or to feel a sense of self ccomplishment.

Planning for skills rather than products

In planning for skills rather than end products
you will find you change what you offer in your
setting and how you view activities. Playdough
becomes a means of developing fine motor
hand and finger strength rather than a way to
make biscuits or snowmen. You set out paint
to print or scrape rather than produce a certain
picture and you add more activities planned
to develop skills such as pouring, scooping,
squeezing and threading rather than those with
a tangible end product. You as a practitioner
begin to see learning as a process and begin to
plan for the process rather than the product.

Praise the process ••••••••

A reminder of what to praise.

Creating & Thinking Critically

Having their own ideas

...an lids and spoons to make music.

Creativity – what is it?

Creativity is not about being able to paint a perfect picture or make an intricate sculpture. It is a way of us as human beings being able to express ourselves in whatever way we feel able. Some may prefer to paint, others sing and dance, while some may build, construct and design. As practitioners in early years we need to make sure that the children in our care can express themselves in their own unique way whenever they feel the need. They need to feel confident to share their ideas and their thoughts and know that we, as the adults, will help them in their quest to turn ideas into reality. No-one ever told Monet, Picasso or Henry Moore to copy someone else's work, so why should we expect children to replicate something we have thought up?

I know I'm being a bit controversial here but doesn't it throw into question the validity of everyone making an identical Christmas card or all painting a sunflower? How creative are our children actually being? Are we displaying creativity or are we creating to display?

To enable true creativity to grow in our children we need to enable our environments to allow children to build, stick, cut, dance, create and sing whenever the mood takes them. Our Creation Stations need to have open access to a wide variety of materials and tools so that children can make what they want when they want. Children need access to wide ranging, open-ended resources such as block play so they can build and invent when they feel the urge. Try offering a CD player and a collection of CD's so that children can explore music, singing and dance at the same time as building their I.T. skills. A small collection of carefully chosen and accessible instruments is likely to be accessed far more readily than loads of instruments in a box.

Small collections of selected instruments.

Outdoor art studio.

Don't forget to make provision for creating outdoors too! A wide variety of loose parts will give many options to design, build and explore. You could even, like us, think about turning an under-used shed into an outdoor studio with more natural resources and a chance for those children who prefer to be outdoors to paint, draw and explore their creative side. A pan, lid and spoon collection offers an amazing chance to explore sound and rhythm outdoors.

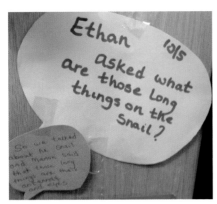
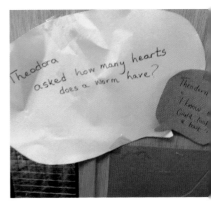

Children's questions offer a sign post to further inquiry and learning.

Giving children a voice

Best practice in early years allows children to work as active partners in the learning process. To have a voice in how and where the learning process goes. Hence, the child le(approach again appears preferable to an environment where the choices about what to learn are made and planned for by adults. This does not mean we just ask children what

…ey want in a florist play area we have decided to build. It needs to show they are truly …volved in the processes and development in as many ways as possible. Planning for …dependence, as discussed previously, allows children to make daily choices about how …ey spend their time and where they want their learning to go.

…o be able to give children a voice within our settings we need also to begin to truly listen …o them. To show them that what they are saying has a real influence on how things work. …y recording their questions and their views to focus practitioner attention on where to …ally take adult input and their support. Encourage practitioners to listen to children's …deas and help them to make them a reality by providing tools and materials to help. Do …ou offer children choices at every point in their day? Can children choose what they play …ith, what they make, how they make and where they go? Are all of our children ebing …stened to regularly? Instead of recording who accessed an activity you planned why not …y recording whenever an adult actually has a two-way conversation with a child? You will …oon pick up on those children whose voices need to be heard more and identify possible …eech and language development issues into the bargain.

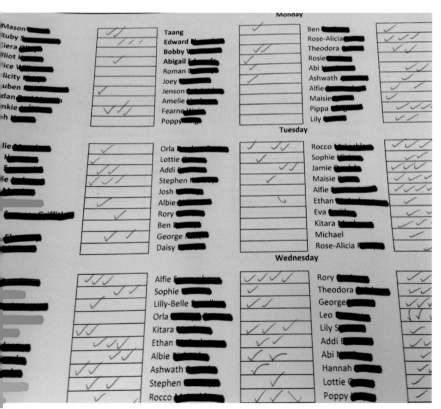

…n example of a conversation tracker.

Access all areas all of the time

Giving children access to both indoors and outdoors at all times is really important if children are to make informed choices about what and where they learn. It should not be restricted to certain times of the day or only in fine weather. Provide outdoor all weather clothing to maximise the choices children have available all year round. Make sure you have appropriate clothing for adults too. The biggest obstacle to children accessing outdoor learning in all weathers is more often than not the adult's reluctance. Remember the weather always looks worse from the inside looking out. Don't forget to spend as much time and thought developing your environment outdoors as well as indoors. As with indoors open ended resources and loose parts are key to offering choice and excitement.

Child led role play

We have already covered the importance of children playing with "what they know", and yet some traditional teaching practices still advocate the need to build a new role play area every few weeks. These are often based around a theme or topic which is adult led and adult-planned. Role play, like all other areas of EYFS should ideally follow the children interests and build on their actual life experiences. Although role play is an integral part of imaginative play and story building, ask yourself how many times a child in your care has actually been to a travel agent or a florist? Remember just because we trailed our cla down the high street to visit the travel agents does not mean it automatically becomes part of their interest and experience. Try to keep any role play development to themes drawn from the children's present interest. If they have enjoyed writing with paper and envelopes then add a post-box, or build a Ben 10 space ship from a box if the play has been all about aliens and space. In these situations, you are **enhancing** and **extending** the play rather than directing it. If you have to have a shop, make it one they visit regular – Tesco and McDonalds offer lots of opportunity to explore healthy eating choices and money in context.

Most of the time a home corner will offer the best way to explore real life and can be enhanced itself rather than changed completely. I advocate always having a home corner even if you decide to also build a café or a car wash too, as these will only last for as long as the children's interest prevails. Wherever possible offer open-ended opportunities for role play as well, where children can make and be whoever they want. If having a reconstructed role play area (one only filled with empty boxes, drapes, tubes and baskets) does not appeal, then try just having a box day. Where you fill indoors or outdoors with empty boxes and see where the children go.

excite...engage...explore...enhance...exten

Making links

Revisiting – enhance and extend

From the offset I have advocated the importance of revisiting learning opportunities to ensure effective learning takes place. Never has it been so important than when children need to make links between what they have already done and what they are about to do. Giving children the chance to try something again. Either repeating their previous success, or changing something slightly, is vital in helping them to build on existing learning and develop the confidence to try things differently and more creatively.

Planning for revisiting, as an integral part of learning, has a huge impact on how we plan over all. It means that we lose the need to plan something different for every day and lends itself to a system where little or no forward planning at the beginning of the week is necessary. Practitioners wait and see what the children are interested in before they decide what to keep, enhance or lose for the next day. Do they choose to reuse it or lose it?

We may start the week with certain enhancements in mind from the previous week but where this week will end up is anyone's guess! Make sure to have space where creations still in process can be stored until they can be revisited and extended. In doing so we show children that we really value their ideas and creations and that "tidy up time" does not automatically bring their adventures to an abrupt end.

Just because we don't plan activities on paper does not mean that we are not planning for learning. If we plan our environment around the children's interests and make it exciting then the learning will come from the children and their inbuilt enthusiasm for exploration and finding out. The bit that we then record is what the children actually did and learned and what they need to have available next time they are in, to be able to revisit and explore learning further.

Use photos to help children revisit their learning.

Photos, displays and the power to revisit

It is not always possible, especially if you are a pack away setting, to keep out what the children were working on during a previous session. This is where the power of photography in helping children to revisit their previous explorations comes into its own. By taking photos of a child or group of children as they explore, and then displaying these the children are able to look back and revisit their previous thinking. Building on their existing knowledge, children begin to make links between what they already know and what they want to do next.

Try having a rethink of your displays within your setting. I believe strongly that display should, as with everything else in an early years setting, serve a purpose in the learning process. Rather than being a labour intensive wallpaper with no purpose other than to make your classroom look good! Using photographs of previous learning as the centre of your displays, not only gives children the chance to look at, discuss and revisit their

Add old display pictures to scrapbooks.

...arning, but also gives a powerful opportunity to show parents and other agencies what ...arning really goes on in the setting. Believe me, Ofsted can tell a lot more about a setting ...om a photo display than they can from sixteen near identical pictures of a tiger on the wall!

...hen using photos to document learning make sure that you change them intermittently ...o that they reflect your current cohort. Hence, the children are able to continuously ...iscuss and revisit thinking and learning which may not currently be happening. When ...ou dismantle your display save the photos and add them to photobooks or scrap books ...nd make them available to children in book areas or near where the learning happened ...o they are available on an ongoing basis.

When an artist came to town ....

Display processes not products

When considering what photos, you are going to display it is important to consider whether it may be more powerful to take multiple pictures, to portray a learning process, than just a single snapshot. The power of documenting a "learning journey" rather than just a "wow moment" has long been a central part of Reggio thinking and has since been adopted as best practice in the UK.

Practitioners need to recognise that learning does not happen in little, one off snap shots and begin to see the bigger picture of an ongoing learning path unfolding in front of them. How you then document this journey will depend upon personal choice. You may choose to display your learning journey on a wall so discussion with other children and parents can occur. Or you may choose to make your observations into a learning journey book. You may even choose to record the learning journey as a series of pictures in the child's learning journal. Some of the current online learning journal facilities allow for multiple photo functions so that this can be done. Sometimes you may choose to annotate the child's thinking and comments, and other times you may just see that the photos tell their own story. The power of pictures to both show children that you value their learning and their ideas as well as showing staff, parents and visitors that learning is an extended process cannot be underestimated.

ake multiple photos to document a learning journey.

An argument for paper based profiles

In a world full of fast moving technology and increasing call for online journals and recording of children's learning, the power of something printed and tangible that children can sit and look at openly and revisit whenever they wish cannot be overlooked. It offers a vital opportunity not only for children to build links in their learning but to build self-confidence and communication skills as they take pride in what they have already achieved and share it with their friends. I also believe that although online recording advocates parental access to learning, many parents still prefer to hold a record of their child's learning in their hand.

...ecording learning journeys.

Choosing ways to do things

Adult role in extended thinking

Obviously all that we have previously looked at with regard to independent access and individual choice in child led learning is central to this area of CoEL. For children to make their own choices and decide on how to do things themselves, they have to be offered the opportunity to do so. Again the adult role moves from being that of teacher and deliverer of information to that of facilitator offering opportunities and support. Adults enhance and extend the children's learning as it naturally develops from their own explorations. They start to see themselves as the support mechanism to the children's ideas, questions and explorations rather than the deliverer of top down information and facts. Ofsted in its recent inspection framework (Ofsted 2015) points out quite clearly that learning is **NOT** a top down process (see display above).

Open ended questioning

To enable learning to move forward adults need to become confident in the use of open ended questioning. Asking questions of children that do not require a yes or no, or one-word answer but that encourage children to explore their own thinking and to begin to think of the endless other possibilities available to them. When using open-ended questions try to make them personal to the children so that they begin to realise quickly that they are allowed their own opinions and ideas. That there are no right or wrong answers. In doing so children begin to value the views of others, even if they differ from their own. Ask questions such as "I wonder what will happen if you...?" Or "what do you think...?". And then as a practitioner, be prepared to help the children follow through on exploring their own thoughts and ideas, rather than dismissing them as incorrect. "Let's see shall we?" or "why don't you try it?" are much more empowering to young children than "I don't think" or even "you can't".

Display open ended questions as staff prompts.

Sometimes in busy learning environments adults become stuck for what to say when a child is mid-invention or engrossed in an investigation. Firstly, ask yourself if you actually need to say anything at all. Will your questioning interfere with the learning or even stop in its tracks? And then if you think you can sensitively enhance their thinking you may find having some open ended questions available as prompts useful. We use the spaces up above child eye-level as adult use zones and fill these with our language and questioning prompts. After all what is more useful running around the top of your walls, a number line that is so high that children never look at it or a means of building staff confidence to talk to children and work together to take learning forward?

Coloured sand mark-making

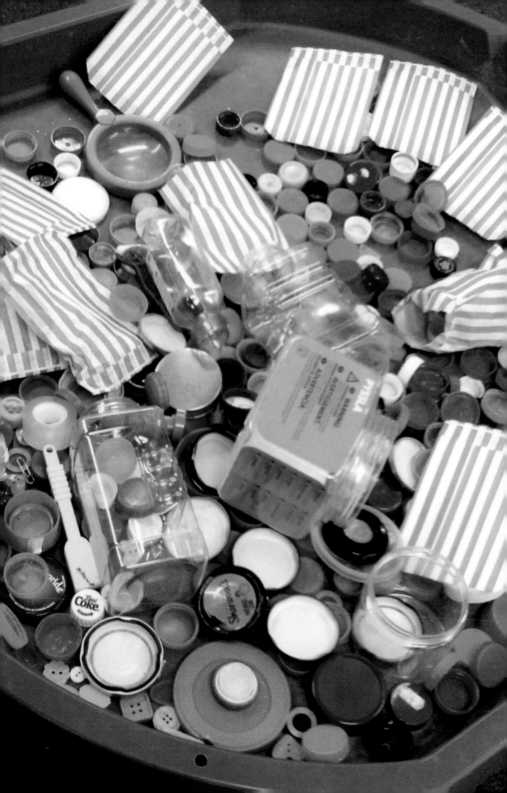

Planning for Child Led Learning

Although this book does not cover the planning process in detail (that's a whole other book!), it is worth a final mention bearing in mind all that has been said previously. A move away from planning activities to planning for child led learning can seem hugely daunting at first. Even more so if we have also chosen to drop the traditional rolling "topic" approach, where dinosaurs are always delivered in the summer and minibeasts are only ever focused on in the spring. Sometimes it's hard to get our heads around the fact that planning for learning in this way looks very different and doesn't require loads of pre-planned paperwork. That does not mean we don't need to do any planning at all. What it does require is that we plan a well-resourced, open-ended environment which stimulates children's interest and builds on their natural curiosity. It then requires us to watch carefully, spot learning where it is happening, record moments when we see learning occur and then build on what we observed to take learning forward. It requires us to **enable, engage, explore, enhance** and **extend,** whilst at all times looking to **excite, excite** and **excite** some more.

What we actually end up doing is planning retrospectively. We observe and record what happened rather than what we think will happen. We spend more time reflecting and less time predicting. We plan the environment rather than the learning outcome. It means we shift our thinking from teaching an activity, where there is only one learning objective, to looking for the learning in whatever the children are interested in doing.

How you record what you observe is down to you. Find something that works for you and your situation, don't feel you have to follow one method or another. As long as you can show the cycle of observation, assessment, reflection and planning, and you are providing evidence that all children are making good progress in their own individual journey to build confidence, skills and knowledge, you are doing what the EYFS requires of you. You children will be, as a result, displaying the Characteristics of Effective Learning within their play and you will hopefully begin to see it and document it now that you have planned for it to happen.

Good luck in your journey towards a child led early years environment and I really hope you enjoy the ride!

excite... engage... explore... enhance... exten